Ives' heart races his vocabulary to the goal in us—
the long arc of his sentences, rainbowing down to
a sudden shock—his lines jolt. Every sentence
leaves us with something we've never known
before, some new giving from the mind embodied
in words. His syntax is a house on fire, and like
flames his words are hungry and quick, and leave
nothing the same after they pass. That's what
draws me to his work—it changes things, it
entrains difference. No poet I know of is so
determined to summon clangorous words from
technologies ancient and future, and so willing to
yield his own huge breath, trained by a lifetime in
music, to their service.

—Robert Kelly, Series Editor

D0917662

wavetable

MICHAEL IVES

wavetable

DR. CICERO BOOKS

Copyright © 2015 Michael Ives
All rights reserved.
Reservados todos os direitos de tradução e adaptação.
Tous droits de traduction, de reproduction et d'adaptation réservés
pour tous les pays.

www.drcicerobooks.com

Dr. Cicero Books
New York Rio de Janeiro Paris
First Edition
Manufactured in the United States of América
Distributed by Small Press Distribution, Berkeley, CA
ISBN: 0692354123
ISBN-13: 978-0692354124

For Mary

Many of the poems contained herein, whether in their current manifestation or in earlier forms, appeared in the following periodicals, to the editors of which I extend abundant thanks:

3rd Bed, 5_Trope, 24, Aufgabe, The Bard Papers, Conjunctions, Facture, First Intensity, Flim, Gargoyle, Hambone, Hunger, Jacket, Lungfull!, New American Writing, New Orleans Review, Nomadics (the blog of Pierre Joris), Octopus, Salt Hill, Seneca Review, Skanky Possum, Sulfur, Unsaid

I would like, as well, to extend my sincerest thanks to Carey Harrison and Dr. Cicero Books, to my colleagues and students at Bard College, and especially to Robert Kelly and Ann Lauterbach for their generous editorial guidance and inestimable friendship.

CONTENTS

No one guards the oasis

The Sphinx's Entrails

Underground Bells

Spem in Alium

From the gland of intention

Skin Weather Memory

No one guards
the oasis

No one guards
the oasis.

At the center
of each grain of sand

an inundation awaits
its signal: zeniths

herding themselves downward
to drink from it

which makes
a dark blossom

where the sky was.
With these drained heavens

will I polish
my detection equipment.

Another eclipse is at hand.
The king's contortionist withdraws.

Complicated thunder spreads
through underground stations.

What *is* the devil's colon?
Path of the typhoon, says the council of the wise.

So much for the wise.
The children turn their faces cloudward.

From their open mouths air raid warnings issue.
Don't you know, Aunt June?

They're the little birdies.
On a wire strung from two

Cheerio-sized muscles
in the face of the horizon

paper-thin strips of the clown
billow in the wind.

We must disenthrall ourselves
to get the thrall we want. Premium

thrall.
Who wants to raze the evidence dome?

This ubiquity is self-defeating.
Space thinks.

Judas didn't just happen.
As a trace element among extremes,

mute delight is
practically rococo.

Air: bliss to one,
cudgel to another.

I have seen the mountains of Valais,
but this country pleases me

more than all those wonders.
Store the new bottles in the old wine.

Abraham was trapped with me
in the seed pod,

which to split open,
required emanations

and a new kind
of brooding.

Maybe he was just
doing his impression

of a living room
lost in the desert:

issue commandments,
preserve the clan,

name son
after water hole.

Arduous overland route
back to a pastoral memory —

what else can a body
do but nectarize

the secretions
of this madness.

How much *now* must extend
beyond the station platform

before a departure
is officially concluded

and the arrival can begin
to press its vanishing point

between fresh layers
of contradiction?

In the time it takes the stationary
to suck flat a bead of ink

a wind path has already written its kingdom
into the beech's flank.

By horses buried in full gallop,
the grave chained to the cradle.

A clean transfer from thought to act
has no hobbies, if staying invisible

doesn't count. Well, and
staring down the task horizon

'til it's a geometric point,
which Euclid defines as

"that which has no part."
The tight space notwithstanding,

it would take a hundred years
to recapture in words

why the witness to the crime
blames himself.

For the abstraction that was
his unmolested field of view

has been ripped open
by his just happening

to be somewhere,
and all the baby spiders

pouring out from behind
make a trail for him to follow

away from his tranquil inner molten-ness
toward a congealed frontier

where swordplay traced against the air
apotheosizes knowledge.

Who's letting whom
build what bomb?

No need to dig up the Urnfields.
New dream controls proliferate.

Wandering like pastoral nomads
they hook a siphon to the gene wave

and forge their beaters.
What *was* ambrosia? Bark? The percept?

Material vows as witnessed by eyes
before receding into their visions?

Air, so strict and precise,
polices, nay, *hath forged* the touch response

by applying to it the anonymity of nerves
that never were.

Then come more Sea Peoples.
Let us return to the tightening coils.

The herd's gyres
leave but divots

in a scum.
Nor will orange

cones falsely
distributed

fool the pursuer.
Dressed as

"The River of Time"
he'll file the

pope in you
to a cutting edge.

Bas-reliefs baked into the shuttle's heat shield
warned us of the price we'd pay.

Large dark bubbles amassed.
It was then I built the vanishing chamber.

"Watkins, I said, "why is the lava corded?"
He handed me a system of sliding rods.

That may have started it,
this inner glaciation, I mean.

With such hazards an ebbing
could very well mistake itself

for a threshold, empty ritual
the dispersion medium in any case.

Thus do we moil in false clay.
And here too, wheels

and forking pipes of suspicious origin.
Electric tables flank the silence.

Life monad
drifts into scar.

Honey place
cannot help

but fall in
with tracking system.

Haunts at the entrance
to a visible heaven

still speak
on behalf of femurs

half out of the mouth
of on behalf of.

And the pepper bird
shall do as it pleases

for there is
no such bird.

Precious stones
void away the anguish.

That's why
the named values intensify

with the breakdown
of complex solids.

Radicalized by fresh
surveillance imperatives,

a window in the dairy case
shatters. That transient

shining body we call flame,
it bids us ask,

Will I too lie soon
upon the cooling board?

Flint knives and copper bracelets;
test ban treaties and shark pavilions:

the days of youth end
in a corridor of echoing beaches.

Thugs are running dog races
in the aqueduct.

All around the plateau,
butch ways of chariotry

loiter, waiting for a warrior caste
to establish itself.

Too early for me to start drawing
broad conclusions from this.

Must resume reconstruction of the star clock.
That, or else disappear into a novelty cocktail.

How far inside these years must I travel
before I need no longer call them mine?

At the gun show
they're selling watermelon sorbet

in hollow plastic bullets.
"This is my death bling," says the death god.

"Touch it. Feel it."
And seeds of the wild lettuce float past.

Blood in the sand,
on the espadrille.

Cries issue
from a tomb.

I mike a tureen
in the villa.

Too much
thinking weather.

Does anyone here remember
getting off the bus?

And how am I to raid
the hollow pillar?

Having no liquid phase
it sublimates

directly into a gas,
going around

calling itself
the deaf balloonist,

Mind, in lieu
of iron phlox

coming up
through its cheek.

The third signal tower fell.
I dropped the implant.

When we came to
we were staring at ears of corn.

All chrome, thirty of them in a row:
grille of the bastard's Town Coupe.

Crazy. I wasn't made for this.
Joanne would be waiting dinner for me.

Flank support had stayed behind
to realign the optics.

Anonymous black two-doors
were crossing the tarmac, as always.

Many are the words for rudder
when the helmsman is no more.

What were we going to do anyway,
issue writs?

Even Senzei was gone
opening a sundries shop in his mind.

Chop water, carry wood,
kill your parents.

The peal
of a slaughter gong

splits the air:
thrust package

delivered.
Grab the hem

of the mental healer.
He agrees

to disagree,
as if imparting

a violent
acceleration

to the impassive
soil, famous

as a death house.
Lightning drives joules

into the screw pine.
Enkindled by a hair-

stroke, worlds
closest-packed.

Quiet as a muffled rape
under the bleachers

the smell of new office space
explains why there's so little B-complex

in so large a bottle.
Were packaging to return

to a dimension commensurate
with its contents

the subtle shock, purring
like a microwaveable twilight

of *Adult Contemporary 103*,
would eat away

the nerves and their sheathing
with its acid

of martyred presidents, of nubby bouclé
and pre-sweetened cereal,

straight through to
the bastardized horse-sacrifice

at the center
of the Protestant night.

Poolings of anonymities leave faces.
Star groups dip out of season.

Crowded together at a window,
the accumulated heedlessness

riveted to an air bridle
blames tools for the ills of men.

Dip him in acid
who loves transfiguration.

The Sphinx's Entrails

dark coasts of memory
        spreading their hordes
                across the stillness in seeds
        tell of another place
    of metals whirlpools tides in the tree ring
        turbulent canopy of oak behind face
                where thought grinds to a dry whisper
        leaf against leaf
                        and black grass is all the eloquence

                              ate the dark gland
                    a thread's width between breaths
        dark breathing   dark thread
              arms two watery histories   legs a swollen cataract of cities
                    between exilic head and foot   blind stele of organs
                          staring in disbelief at this tide of impermanence
                    christens one stream life   the other death
              from their fork pulls a tale
        that devours its young

mind an ergot on blown grain   always recursus   to original dilemma
      the divided human   rhythm unchanging   unforgiven
to run fruitless   natural definition of inherited bondage   must dance
      must dance   elsewhere (is care)   browsing on a decayed canopy
mind a blight, etc.   in ninth month swallowed bitter ropewater
      broken cups and wests   grew to manhood   arrived at this ravine
dug from the waiting   and dominion over herds of torn sentences
      now sprinkle these last drops of   unmixed no one   in Thracian
fashion over the ground   do not drink   ground

returned as fast   was all the warm year
   drove down to that horrible water
     looked away
             no shame more   for that I gave you
              the dying year   held its face under water
      its eyes
        full of coasts beyond words   gone
                         gone into the end
                             less wave

ran once my index through a vertical beam of light
fearsomely aglow come down silent
for to announce it was there in a wilderness alone
cared little beseems but my finger smearing it across at horizontals
by this swipe I let a way for it to cantilate
made the manner of its song
to enter my eyes and wash away
the chrism of lensical behoove
which makes us mulish and obedient

water   it will spell you
                    empty syllables
                                    may as soon
            speak into mirrors   possesses nothing so much
                        as a wiser
                                    soullessness
                        than itself
            nor for any sake   its bones
                                    an unremembered ice

all this world devoured
along the path of its appearance
as it was seen understood
eaten then forgotten
for another world
not larger but close to hand
whether animal herb
this or that gathering force
against which this herb this animal
is forgotten for something separate
in a word but consubstantial this vastation
and again we are *in* rather than *are*
we it is
we are devoured

that something as I walked struggled to escape speak
though as to what constituted its words were penned in
        I could not say whether by beings laws memories but such a one
communicated whose vital parts shared a unique moment
        in space with mine I have determined by following
an unexplained filament under the skin
        from the midriff down to the distinct impression a woman
bides with me yet upside down with respect to a vertical orientation
        is more than a fond surmise that relative
to a dorso-ventral axis she would disbutton
        along my spine to reveal her breasts to the oaks at my back

every animal that is in someone wants explaining
      parts flames twists no one can say   are pieces of one
        is exactly oneself   that want
    in rooms of one person   is blood of a new animal   flowing
      through the dream of another animal's blood
          so I in you   as clouds cross from a preceding day
           part of someone   that exactly
        not one piece but flames
      to tell you I am in you   is my want
for no way you will know you are in me exactly   is a music
                              no one can know

to walk into a bird's eye must concede
a person as good as already entered and left that
        dark portal often enough a bird's eye be our
own come through the door of our vision or else
        a figment this palace of beasts looking at us looking
at them looking and where haven'tly we dwell by our
        insistence the beast element resolve into speech and
high discrimination whenas fisheye give onto birdeye give onto
waterdrop give onto debris ring give onto zed give onto omicron give
onto amphoramouth give onto manmouth give onto womanmouth
give onto congruentwith give onto sameas give onto giveonto

so soon dispatched
> against the tide of appearance
> the fine work of faces
> ground smooth
eyes and mouth paved over
> a Cycladic anonymity feathered
> into the mid-channel
> of the body's remembered
> Jacob

flooded with sun storms   orions and wandering sand letters
        among herring in low riot of pewter
                their stilled eyes stalking another sirius
                      father in a box   having answered for my crimes
                          was pulled into the water's face
                  glinting with surface novas
            among sinuous dark pantomimes
        my lineaments rippled
and were replaced

pillar

of

salt

of

dense

silence

of

the

wise

ones

dissolves

Underground
Bells

Crowd of Swiss villagers with torches searching for ugly guy
made out of lots of parts of other slightly handsomer guys
or only handsomer outside but uglier inside because
they aren't made of parts of other guys but really are
except they don't know it which makes them uglier inside
but makes the fact of that inside ugliness less important
than being slightly handsomer outside.

From fees and little welts, this go-to consciousness
with minty-fresh breath and investment bankers for sensory neurons.

Carried I my volatile grievance in a velvet-lined casket.

The committee said, "Let us hear your grievance."

I opened the casket and removed the flask.

The committee said, "How could you, who bring grievance, afford such a casket?"

"If you would, please," said I, "I would air my grievance."

"What of the casket? Where did you get it? Did you steal it?"

"This is my grievance, here in this flask. What matter, the casket?"

"I shouldn't be so sure of myself, were I lowly as you, and come into possession of such a casket as that."

Thus became the grievance the thing it was carried in.

(Consider next the Buprestid slow-explosion beetle)

which ingested by the pasturing cow poisons and causes to swell
the drowsy animal lets into its house of intricate order
a righteous Judith lures then beheads her arrogant expectant
Holofernes or "spatial extension"
though the serpent "tastes" such threats molecule by molecule
by means of its Jacobson's organ
for all ambiguities shall eventually be resolved
all tyrannies choked in their own coils
and the sky shall hide beneath the earth
and steal our thoughts from those underground bells
our bones.

The selves are not oriented vertically. They do not stand upright.
The selves rest in loose bands along the surface, slide under
and over, follow gradients, gather at pulse points scattered across.
The selves are migrants, yet they take no wage from the harvest.
They drift through permeable membranes along their way.
Some of their number mingle with the Circean salts of persons,
refuse to leave the compound. Tearful partings of ways
leave a rime at the cheek, destination of pilgrimages. And it begins.

The selves are not our selves.

(The McMartin preschool case)

The brilliant clarity of water was long presumed void
of all but varieties of limpidity: stillness, concentric
fluctuation, form within flow as of liquid thought,
yet, put to lens, proved dense
with the translucent sides of animalcules, which,
barely more than a thickening of the water's motive, still,
when measured against the membrane of the concept,
appear wholly opaque, as is said also of the obtuseness of angels,
through whose wings the finer variants of light shall never pass.

(Between ecstasies)

Riding herd with you at night along a Hentai spillway
toward the precious soul module
where boy fevers and butane impinge
strange children flipping the light on and off
force open all these hairline fissures
we've stuffed with a roaming around
waiting for the drugs to arrive shall likely
bring harsh blows against our foreheads upon the morrow
bending down to reach for all that free money
and it's never where it says it is
neither morrow nor money all the livelong summer
ground into a powder of morning ragas.

My supine person makes a sluice through the insects' cadence.

A bird near a stone portends flight, yet a stone under a bird
   is but a stone.

The tasks of the shade multiply, for I smoke the leaf my name,
   and an ash colored with suspicion collects at the end of the
   vanward segment.

These macular and degenerative summers catching along the old pier
   sidle to a rhythm no one can duplicate.

Such is the dance, into which the dancers enter, holding their noses,
   which is part of the dance.

Cling to me only with thine cold cash.

I will herd the cattle of the sun into the abattoir of the moon,
   and grill the light energy steak to the stars
   on my dark matter hibachi.

(Auricle)

Full of a nut-black persistence to wear a living garment –
composed, the greater part of it, of sound – it happened
that I came once to a hovering dome of bees,
which from a distance appeared the size of a great stadium,
yet upon approach proved no larger than a helmet,
but composed, for all that diminution, of the same
great number of bees. To place it over my head,
I conjectured, would demonstrate, after its removal,
what an apiary of wisdom silence is.

Chemical estuaries – visited by
no animal, no sun, no moon, but only
reflections of moons, suns – enpulp
the brain guava, girdled in a thinking latex.
We lay boughs before it, as before
all the clever fruits, to propitiate
its quench and motor savvy.
For it doth teach us to blow the eider down away.
For it doth butcher the eider.

(Song explained)

Cravings advertise themselves as riches,
yet are loath to be had, or else would,
but in so doing, perish on the way, and split thus,
like us they wreck themselves on that distinction.
For nothing wants to be the possession of another,
yet, as a treasure beyond words to the self that wants it so,
to *be* is to be *owned*, and further, *used* to ends, against which,
in the more general end, a thing has no weapon
other than its nullity, which makes a melody.

Humans in cars: an evolutionary
devolution toward the insectile,
steel outer body a chitonous check
against the perilous hopes
of the daughter-in-law
who leaves signs of her menstruation
in the father's bedclothes
to chant his son away
from not waking.

Your last breath shall be your truest flower,
burst up triumphant
out of its analogue to sleep,
shake free the accumulated muck,
its seedcase break within you
and a liberated festival of nerves
shoot like fissures in a windshield
across the vast sudden final countenance of this life,
rippling with scenes of god birth
and unendurable ecstasy.

Spem in Alium

Wreckyear the dry wind the turgor gone all that you cherish

Darkening waterlessness bent over its one hand its eyes turned in against Hope in the corner splashes in the petroleum flowerets in ruined buildings the fluorocarbons the blood-jazz aquarelles coiling in lymph between whirling blades she

Murmurs in autistic repetition the revealed edge the creche of words in her venom sack her eyes tell

Her eyes the empty orbits the iris of Hope collapsed like a tissue against bramble growing

Through a bramble growing out where once the eyes of Hope a dog in chains its gnashing teeth out of all proportion to the rest of it harrowing the earth below the thorn these

Teeth this shuddering muscle and fur in chains to the bleached horizon out of her orbits two inextricable beams of chain and

A trawl of scars down her cheeks it spells the darkening and the bombs the secret writing of grimaces it flickers along the scarred hollows in time to

To the ting and snap of the chain the whipping feral clumps dragged out of her brambled orbits enchained hounds hauled out of the skull of Hope cornered murmuring and freaked over with knotted shakes of saliva the secret writing

The revealed edge the promise to raze tomorrow with fire all that I cherish I merge with the bullet-headed future passions the dark tailings of reminiscence to bring this shell game of sacred previsions to an end

Of life was hopelessly strewn it gathers in the bullet will bring the shall-it-be game shell comes to a complete
Stop all the gannet-winged maps to the wilder parts to the gethsemani of scars across her cheek for the forked warning goes as it kevels and if

I fall promise to

Raze it tomorrow with fire all that I cherish it goes as it kevels it goes over the darkening the cattle of all innocence I prayed and was reshackled to the darkening parts the whirling blades out in the interknitted passions the dark tailings the reminiscence now that it begins to rain for the last cattle of all innocence driven into a grove of whirling blades out in the interknitting in final rain and the bombs the tailings we coupled near on broken glass eyeless Hope and I for the last finish on then the old darkening march of reminiscences cattle of all memory driven into a grove and riven the untabulated bitten into I pray as it goes all the untabulated life

I am darkening I am sleeked over with darkening my eyes rain for the last time

(Empire)

At the head
of a midrib
flume between
heavily veined
shoulders where
rainwater beads
huge, in
queues of clear
ovate knobs
advancing at
uneven intervals
a single droplet
waxes 'til it can
no longer resist
the gradient
and peels off
from its wedging
grows like a
crowd as it
overtakes its
lower neighbors
and at the leaf
tip, with
reluctance and
growing larger
still, plunges
and breaks into
multitudes
over the iliac
crest, some
of these arrivistes
trickling down
buttockward
into a mash

of fern
and broadleaf
others recollecting
themselves in
fresh congress
along the circuitry
of my pubic
whorls finding
their liquid way
into the loose
ripple of sheen
laid along
the after wake
as I comb slowly
again and again
lovingly the slick
rondure of your
freshly detached
head these
droplets of water
suffering their
final disintegrative
communion
as they pass
out of reluctance
into general
glistening.

(The grain that hurries this way)

Along the tasseled
animal spine —
turning her
dream away
from the salt gardens'
leaves, from
the holothurian,
the black rocks —
a now approaches.
Through innumerable doors
it shuttles, down
hallways lined
with attendants
to whom it is
oblivious —
they stand
so still — as if
the now, coming
to relieve us
of memory,
were passing
through ribs
of some huge beast
longer than length
itself. Finally, though,
the grass takes
everything into *its*
singular indifference,
even the now,
a distillation
of grass.
The clock
of the grass
will transect

then swallow
your most private
mesopotamia
in its arms.
Slow and huge,
the arms
of the grass
lumber hidden
like muskellunges
under the dill
and thyme.
How they must
narrow themselves
to occur to us!
How often we
mistake the grass
for our feet,
for the will
of the feet,
for a purpose,
sufficient to
fur the pulsations
of memory
into a stillness
pelted out
beyond the drug
of movement
toward despair,
which is granular
and hisses.

(Standing one's ground)   *(in Sanford, FL)*

But animals *are* machines
until one of the higher-ups changes the rules
which old order we have always already agreed must suffice
whether their movements be rapid
linear or circular
their will to live
serrated with suspicious clothes
as to their *use* in *this* neighborhood
defined by *our* superior presence within it
a regeneration of their organs
could possibly justify their distance
from our immediate need
why go to the trouble
to clear an ultimate ground of dignity
we're not the ones squirting the venom
how could it possibly matter
that our signs are a private preserve
all our own
powers must be *discovered*
and the satisfactions running parallel to an unavoidable victimage
all the while determine
the reach of sovereignty
between which hardened categories
the civilized brain's cocaine is ground
will require a few more centuries
to quell these insurrections
among the floors.

(Gulf stream)

Who shall consider the cuckold
his movement through space
in proportion as he hates himself
while following her
his tormentor
through the rooms of his house
he would be avenged
though he stare at the back of her head
how in the coming days he imagines his requital
a most fitting *auto-da-fe*
her face by his own hands
twisted around into alignment
with the zipper of her dress
polluted and unrepentant visage
a dual wake feathers behind her of displaced air
she passes all understanding
he shall follow behind her all the days of his life
the air through which he moves thick with minute knives
she will not look him in the face
a son witnesses the two as they pass
his mother walking as if to step out of a garment
his father an impotent persistence
the son falls in behind them
a turbulence of minute knives gathers
mounts behind his father's head
mano cornuta like an impala's
the boy bends one way then another in good shift
but cannot avoid
they shoal in an oxbow formation around his mother
dual wake of knives in vortices closing in behind her
make an envelope of shame around the husband
behind whom a geometrical increase in turbulence
horns rise grand as an impala's from his head
great swarms of trailing knives

ripple and convolve in dense spirals
elaborate with imputation
tell of empires
of intricate obscure grievance
as cuts to the boy's face and breast
ever unable to say who or what cuts him
for all the swarming
his anguish will not betray an original
it must lie with some fault of his own
traceless wounds
unaccountable weather.

(Last words of Serge Chaloff, saxophonist)

Quills dive
where the
open skin
whispers.
Hidden summer,
the mutilationist,
runs away
as the visible
one wrapped
in belts
approaches, quivering
from underneath,
with swans
in the whites
of its eyes.
Hidden one
then belted
one — this
way the
halves of
summer power
its lung,
up into which
like candlepins
junk fantasies
of swans' necks
push their
music — it
is a tithe
paid to
brutality,
whipping its
legs — and
by a confidence

purchased
long ago,
the summer
breathes, a
second music
scored along
the flanks
of the first, the
unbreathing.

Every nerve
grows near,
convinced of
something from
the blood wells
down, a
tear line
of river
flowing from
the saboteur's
mouth.
The stars quiver too
in their flasks
like imperfectly
drugged animals,
all their soft
tunnels of mind
and feeling
caught
in an effort
of expulsion,
as moon lime
pulls the
shrieking lake
down
into an alien
medulla

and a swan's
cry sews me
into the smoke
of burning plastic –
what makes
the ground
wine to rise
in its brother
and hate it,
what makes
the skin
whisper
and open.

(From the private thought worlds of the sons of remote fathers)

Hidden away
in the lung book
of certain air-breathing
spiders a Forbidden
City of "winged words"
his mouthparts
fused over
brittle stars
pictures his parents'
heads diced cleanly
by a vibratile cage
as of cheese-cutting wires
from between
the neat cubes
all that messy
intercellular
verklärte nacht
guttering out onto
the dining room table
hale oh vengeful juju
joins a fugitive
urine let go
in his neighbor's
pool the yellow
string through
his tiny spigot
streams out into the trans-
parent pimpernels
of chlorination
close round
the warming saffron
effluent grabs at his

must hold his
pure product his
voluptuous water
escapes.

(Church fire)

Sidewise screamed across how / went again in pursuit of their / went
heedlessly believing they / all their naked forkings how / harvested the
throat of silence how

Removed the sealed canopic throat in / pulse along the wood how /
seed of what could follow fixed / very longitudes of flame unfurled
across / of speech refused to

Bit into the wood believed in / became many at the shirred edges of /
wood the Janus-roots of flame screaming naked find / and seize upon
all they burn how sow

The seed of / noctivagant fire-knot in full clench with / their stolen
holy throat trailing behind them return to / themselves chew into the
/ pretender the

Imperforate noon at night of / sub-suns of flame-muzzled spurways of
crosses only / naked they believe into the body of fire flows into /
dethroat the wood the pretender

Sowing the heedlessness of / fire biting into it / their / believing

From the gland
of intention

(A secret history of representation)

Personal god plunges fist
Into chest pulls out heart shows
It to his brother shame
Says take eat shame snatches
Heart from hand
Of personal god begins
To take bites from
Shares heart with personal god
Likes what he tastes

The two of them feast on heart is
Fairly devoured blood
All over everywhere but
For that remaining in body
Pools and thickens
For lack of anything to conduct it
Which lack shame
And personal god realize mess
They've made gravity of situation

Take Polaroid of bloody everywhere
Nail it to place where heart was being
Their attempt to correct things
Hurry to get out
Of there shame its sense
Of propriety in hurry
Scribbles under Polaroid
This is not a heart and shame
And personal god depart

Once we thought we'd live
along the peaceable grid
of the paper cutter
under a jungle gym dusk
plaited with contrails.

But we don't. We live here
in a subordinate clause
that says we're only technically awake.

A single glance confirms
the compressed Atlantic between us.

Never saw the moon
leave the horizon.
For it was altogether

too long assumed
by men of that day.
That to them who farmed

remote quarters.
The customs imposts
thereof. I must

bring the Victoria's
Secret Poems to conclusion.
Her highness secretes

a pheromone blend.
From the gland
of intention.

Through a series
of permeable membranes.
Bordering the other Egypt.

Hidden among dream waste
and opioid ampoules.
The electronics in the system

cool under ferns.
They promise nothing.
And ebony. Thing.

Glyphs chiseled into my need to know
conjugate the adjacent desert
like a hinge on the door into a waterfall,

while a millennial rime of oaths
flashes below the rim
and the dark chord turns away.

Though fire shall pour from the locks in its mouth,
in the larger scheme,
blinking with fierceness,

I dovetail into the thing you've become,
issuing from speakers
at an undeclared circumference,

and in calling it to accounts, our lives,
as the air through which it propagates,
tear open a new harbor.

Hence walls, disappearing bookcases,
the carboy filled with a volatile liquid,
night glowing with the albedo

of swans in congress.
Someone's hands roll a carpet
down from the elevated

and blood red lake.
But the hand without a master
disassembles the breathing weapon.

Snowdrop the sex slave undresses
behind the eye patch of the cyborg.
The bathwater cools.

The sentence beginning, "Has
the sentence begun —" begins.

A thunder god's teeth close
'round the sky-father's penis.

Shopping becomes a language.
You must beat your time-shares
into bus tours.

Into her ankle vein
she injects the rage of the hour.
Her mother, hands at her temples, cries,
What has become of my little Destiny?

It's all a rhythm, from the shutting earth
and its buried daughter
to flow of reuptake inhibitor
into the targeted synaptic cleft.

Access to the soft loan window
tightens by the hour.

Controlled, adrenalized,
we survive these auroras.

Before, nothing but the imposition
of untrammeled sound. Soon after,
sight. And only then, as a barrier to the audible,
an offering of hands, modeled on the eyelid,
as the eyelid was modeled after sleep, that antique jetty
lowered against the tide of the sensual incursion.

How stupid, though, stopping the ears with one's hands.
How Rube Goldberg, putting one's hands over anything,

trying to cover anything

Denser than bristles on a hairbrush,
this thickening of time into persons
at nodal points along the way.

I speak someone else's words,
breathe from a shared lung.
Whose eyes have I swollen?

At the beginning of each breath
all the deer in the deer park
look up. What do they see?

Thread of smoke from totem meal
set among thrones.
On the morning of the journey,

Valor and Certitude
feed their mounts
the forbidden supplement,

watching mutely on
as butterflies accumulate
in the grilles of Peterbilts.

Inside

the original
of anything
famished
satyrs
are eating
their
way

out.

Skin Weather
Memory

More ambitious
than a container
gardening project
yet never quite rising
to the level of farmhands
mounting a fireworks display
for the orphanage,
these novel sensations
of the complex sentence
radiate outward
along a wire
reputed to run through
a statistical average
of objects
in the material
universe, till it fray
dangerously
near the silent man
who stands always
to the right of an antique
farm implement,
whether he stands there
or not, pointing
in the direction of
these small cabins
made of words,
built to reveal the valley
that hides them,
known as The Poem,
slanted against its dusk,
preoccupied
with sunsets
and coelacanths.

(Rods and cones)

Given-ness, that
long-form tantrum
of metaphysical
entitlement, integral
to the warmth
of the *because*-relation,
accelerates our forgetting
the radical jujitsu
required to maintain
our faith in
not exactly reality
but the fragile hovercraft of meaning
trapped between
how we distinguish
the modes of the real
from the moment
through which it passes
in thought on its route
through to a non-conceptual event
inverted in all the million facets
of a feeling's eye.

(Higgs boson)

We put into
the harbor, birth
secreted among reeds

by a mother
and live this
tomography of moments

neither possessed
nor relinquished
leviathans cruising

the edge
of early maps
as the discovery

of longitude
wanders through a pulsar
at that irrevocable hour —

thread of staircase
opening to great ages
falling away

from the tensity of me
into and into
rind of the instantaneous

breathing as of now
then again now
round a center

enjoys without blemish
extravagant debauch
compressed to a drop.

(Written to Wayne Shorter's "Teru")

Park mist
gathered
to a four-note
figure

fades
into sepals
a soughing
modulation

of influent
love days
pressed
to the lip

this sometime
quiet
threaded into
a walking thing

that gives
it tells
it is
a self-

knowing
mist in
motion
remote from

loss it
pauses
after the
ebbing night-

organ machinery
of stresses
from ultima
down toward

small of
back and
away in
a mist.   *for Mary*

(Arethusa)

If an unbroken
thread
of milk
should terminate
at the point
of its efflux
into the infant's
mouth the nipple
then understood
as the child
of the milk
which to pull
away from its
source

By a coordinated
effort of child
and breast
is itself
the true milk

If a milk
breaking into
hardened splinters
at the saying
of its source

If it feed
no one

If to live
is to be
drunk
with it

Cool alpine dimension
the air clear
tree, shrub, berry

crisp against
the outward surging tips
of mountains.

Life here has raised itself slowly
into its stark provision
by inches

extended along
a gnarled chain of calculations,
to toe brute peril

the substance of its fate.
Severe, the increment
of reach, and lowly

at extreme heights,
where even the meanest
creeping root

dignifies itself
along a scale of inches
dearly earned.

Precipices themselves breathe
in bright inscrutabilities
only their neighbors can

forge into a cold
approximation of understanding.
The impossible frugality

to which they are consigned
by remote impulses
confers on them

the appearance
of an eternal undertaking
beyond the superfluities of speech.

(Skin Weather Memory)

day breaks the hour's
yolk on night's rim
grows into a spark

sleeps dreams day
enters dream rapidly
drinks itself into

knowing it sleeps
day does slide into
late form of previous

skin weather memory
you call it what slides
into its broken hours

sleeps dreams never
wholly itself as night
alone not another

modus of passing time
breaks bread knowing
day as not night

Single
grain
of
diatomaceous
earth
culled
from
endless
chalk
cliffs:
shored
billions
of the
split
animals'
bones:
diatom:
or
cleaved
across:
rides
its
infinitesimal
fate
into
tinder
compounds
at
the
head
of
a
match
these
paltry
bones
moored

against
renewing
the
Romes
burn
the
babies
cry
life: briefest
of
protectorates.

(Windowed Monads)

Pulsatile, indeterminate : and overlapping occasions : *are* the atoms : arrayed momently in upward spirals : of the lesser kudu : its horn : an harmonic discharge thrust out : glory so shall grow : from its head : uncontended : along the pure flame of animal form : such audacities deposited against, or as : an impulse of horsemen : galloping through the etymological drift : to neither conquest *nor* turbulence : need we resign ourselves : nor to the fate of our conceptions : these atoms : whether hearse or comet, their interior nature : so to approximate the flow : across remotions of space : arcing, expend themselves in great flashes and chains : at spate : over the helio-cliff : in fluid arrangement : its warp the god : in a vortex of water : whose whorl, whose enjoyment without blemish : makes of time the inner nerve of glory : be whatsoever baroque ambition funneled through : brief incarnations : the rock shelves, the actual sea : gush of agate : loosed : into the palm of the eye.

A scattered kentledge
we archipelagoes

of echo and rust
sun systems distant

from a bestial
contentment

the ash flakes
of whose fire

we mount
and equestrianize

our way into a light
shall carry us

off along
weathery paraphs

written through stonechat
and hell heaven

as much as a coombe
through high awful places

which leadeth us
into mentations.

Into this sleep
a winter
wheat raiding
its contentment
soundlessly
and depth
understood
along the shallow
interpenetration
of cloud and memory
you and the eucalyptic
moment never
to be doubted
the completed you
as of your own telling
of semiliquid
tones half-circles
ornate panels
of time between
claims redoubled
over your
sleeping body
the mesenteric blue
you of one
interradial dream.   *for Mary*

Michael Ives is a writer, musician, and sound/text performer living in the Hudson Valley. His poetry and fiction have appeared in numerous magazines and journals in the United States and abroad. His is the author of *The External Combustion Engine*, (Futurepoem) and has taught in the Written Arts Program at Bard College since 2003.

Charlotte Mandell

To the memory of my beloved mentor, the distinguished Brazilian educator, Dr. Emanuel Cicero, born in 1907 in Ubatuba, São Paulo. Rector of the College of Rio Grande do Sul from 1943 to 1978, he died in 1988 in Lisbon.

—Maximiliano Reyes, publisher

-FIM-

DR. CICERO BOOKS